# Self-Esteem

A Comprehensive Manual For Enhancing Self-esteem, Fostering Self Confidence, And Conquering Timidity And Self-Indecision Among Both Genders

*(Enhancing Confidence Levels And Elevating Self Esteem: Strategies And Techniques)*

**Benito Marks**

# TABLE OF CONTENT

Techniques For Increasing Self-Assurance ......... 1

Typical People With High Emotional Intelligence .................................................................. 37

Because Of Your Food .............................................. 62

Managing Unfavorable Thoughts ........................ 69

Techniques For Mitigating Fears And Insecurities By Engaging In Immersive Real-Life Encounters. ........................................................... 92

Strategies For Overcoming Negative Thinking ........................................................................................ 141

# Techniques For Increasing Self-Assurance

I will now proceed to provide a concise exposition of the uncomplicated methods to cultivate and incorporate self-assurance in your daily routine, which can be readily assimilated into your present lifestyle. Do not misconstrue their simplicity. These methodologies can yield significant impacts on your overall experience.

The Significance of Internal Dialogue

Prior to discussing techniques, it is essential to address the significance of "self-talk." As previously indicated, the language one employs to describe oneself, others, and one's circumstances directly influences the standard of life one will experience. If you have previously not been made aware of this information, please refrain from blaming yourself. I, too, remained unaware of it for the initial 42 years of my own experience. It is imperative that you commence fostering belief in the statements I have just made. It is imperative to comprehend that each individual exists within an expansive energy field that actively corresponds to and is influenced by vibrational waves. It is essential to acknowledge that one's speech serves as a transmission center, emitting radio waves that not only propagate outward but also draw towards them analogous frequencies within this field. Adverse language gives rise to an unfavorable existence. Positive vocabulary leads to a constructive and uplifting encounter. Both Buddha and Jesus expounded upon the profound impact of our words, capable of both construction and obliteration, emphasizing the imperative to exercise caution in our selection of language. Hence, it is crucial not to simply disregard this proposition, as it constitutes a pivotal element in facilitating transformation.

Flash-Cards

Pre-constructed affirmation flashcards provide a remarkable means of effectively challenging ingrained patterns of negative self-dialogue. By conveniently keeping these cards nearby, individuals can readily substitute initial negative thought patterns with the empowering and uplifting affirmations inscribed on the cards.

The utilization of flashcards presents a straightforward and uncomplicated approach to facilitate transformation, all while maintaining a high level of efficacy.

Technique Instructions:

Initially, it is imperative to allocate a significant amount of time to introspection regarding the individual you aspire to evolve into, or how you aim to shape your self-perception. Subsequently, diligently transcribe all these reflections. Subsequently, it will be advisable to transcribe those thoughts into individual affirmations, following the aforementioned method, for instance, stating "I possess a fearless and assured demeanor."

In conclusion, ensure that you keep those flash-cards handy and retrieve them whenever you detect any instances of self-deprecating thoughts. Alleviate your thoughts by engaging in meditation and focusing your attention on any of the statements found on your flash-cards. If you articulate them consistently, preferably out loud, it would be even more effective.

Journaling

Now consider how you can utilize that sacred gateway and physiological phenomenon for your advantage. Consider the potential transformation of your thoughts, emotions, and actions through the consistent practice of dedicating time to journaling and reflecting on chosen ideas.

Keeping a personal journal proves to be highly beneficial and transformative, making it an invaluable practice.

When failure strikes

It is highly improbable that you will be fortunate enough to avoid experiencing disappointment throughout the course of your life. In any case, you

One should acknowledge that it is an integral aspect of existence. These are the instances when a profound sense of disillusionment permeates.

Engulfed by ambiguity, your mind becomes challenged in piecing together the certainty you previously acquired amidst the entirety of the situation.

while. You must not let go of your commitment, no matter how unsettled you may be by disillusionment.

ment. In all honesty, any adversity ought to serve as an impetus for you to redouble your resolve and strive earnestly to achieve your goals.

Arrive at your intended destination. In order for this to transpire, condition your mind to cultivate your composure.

and fearlessness. Every step taken towards gaining self-confidence eliminates doubt, leading you back to your path of success once again.

Healthy doubt

It is important to consider that a certain degree of skepticism can be advantageous in acquiring understanding or achievements.

Continuous growth and development experienced throughout the course of one's life. However, when it becomes a factor contributing to your decline

Furthermore, latency can manifest as an eccentric stumbling block impeding your progress towards your objective.

Utilize your inner strength in order to bolster your mental resilience. It is imperative that you strengthen your determination to succeed under any circumstances and undermine any doubts through every possible method available, thus

You will experience a life filled with contentment.

You have the potential to achieve success despite your uncertainties or notwithstanding your uncertainties. Alternatively, you

One might need to recognize the inescapable circumstances and negotiate with whichever outcome appears most severe.

Conceivable option that arises. In the event that this situation arises, it is advised to alter your course, re-energize your resources, and embark on a revised path. Conquer uncertainty prior to its conquest over you.

Overcoming feelings of helplessness

Collectively, we all experience a sense of powerlessness to some extent at various points throughout our lives.

In our existence, this circumstance is acceptable so long as we redirect our attention and conquer these sentiments. Anyway for certain, sen

Feelings of powerlessness ensue and begin to shape our outlook and existence. Here are some

Valuable suggestions to facilitate your comprehension of those emotions of powerlessness and techniques to navigate through them.

quer them.

• Commence by acknowledging the concerns, apprehensions, obstacles, and impediments that evoke your emotions.

Feeling devoid of power and striving to understand the reasons behind these emotions.

• Devote effort towards adopting new beliefs that instill a sense of liberation and fearlessness.

and possess the capability to effectively handle any subsequent outcomes

• Gain knowledge of strategies to effectively address these feelings of vulnerability as they arise

• Employ strategies for effectively addressing conflicts and fostering analytical thinking during their occurrence.

• In the event of experiencing backsliding and feelings of doubt resurfacing, it is important to remember that such occurrences are common and should be faced head-on in order to regain your sense of strength and purpose.

according to the most recent identifiable point of relevance

• No matter how small the achievement, be sure to reward yourself nonetheless.

• Acknowledge that altering our thoughts will necessitate a certain amount of time

Persistently strive towards your goals while embracing vulnerability.

• Strive for excellence, but remember that no one is infallible and we all make mistakes.

• Determine the necessary measures to enhance one's aptitude for self-adjustment and self-recovery.

and fearlessness

Feelings of vulnerability can give rise to various difficulties in life, the

The greater the sense of vulnerability you experience, the diminished your control over your own life becomes; provided below are several regular occurrences.

instances of happenstance arising from a sense of powerlessness.

- You begin to experience an overwhelming sense that no matter your efforts or the extent of your attempts, success remains unattainable.

throughout everyday life

- You develop an excessive reliance on the assistance of those in your vicinity to aid you in overcoming your adversaries.

issues

- It is your conviction that you possess an innate lack of coordination.

- One develops a deep-seated anxiety that one is incapable of managing a situation.

- A sense of despondency and sorrow engulfs you as you navigate through your daily existence, leading to a pervasive feeling of gloom.

- You perceive yourself as an unfortunate individual who consistently requires safeguarding.

circumstances

- Overall, your perspective appears to be characterized by cynicism.

- There is a possibility that you are concerned about how others perceive you as delicate and weak.

- You experience discouragement due to a lack of individuals with whom you can collaborate.

We are pleased to provide assistance by addressing and resolving any concerns you may have.

• You accept the fact that you will perpetually remain vulnerable, and that you are unable to resist or overcome the situation.

under no circumstances alter

There are a variety of ways in which you can aid yourself in overcoming these emotions, highlighting the importance

One important point to remember is that you are not alone, and you can take ownership again.

In order to address your concerns effectively, it is imperative that you reevaluate your lifestyle and make impactful decisions once more. All

All that is required of you is to possess unwavering self-assurance and delve deeply within yourself to discover that resolute confidence.

Transport it to the top. While it is possible for us collectively to overcome our challenges independently, it is not detrimental.

Seek advice from acquaintances and relatives without relying solely on them to solve your problems on your behalf.

Safeguard and Uphold Your Energy

It is crucial that you acquire the ability to conserve and safeguard your energy as an individual with empathic abilities. Having the ability to disengage occasionally from the external world in order to allocate time for personal rejuvenation holds significant importance. An effective method to accomplish this goal is by acquiring a reputable pair of noise-cancelling headphones and utilizing them when venturing into public spaces or encountering noisy surroundings. Although it may not be achievable on every occasion, employing them in specific situations can aid in maintaining concentration on the musical energy rather than the surrounding environment. Please consider incorporating music that is characterized by its uplifting and lively qualities, as it will effectively enhance your energy levels, contrasting with the potential exhaustion that may result from engaging in activities outside the home.

An alternative approach to safeguarding your energy involves initiating the practice of establishing energetic boundaries. This implies that you render yourself unattainable to attune with the vibrations of those in your vicinity, unless you grant yourself explicit consent to do so. Establish a personal barrier whereby you abstain from attuning to any form of energy.

Acquiring the skill to activate and deactivate your talent may require training, and the most effective approach to achieve this is to initiate the process. In due course, you will acquire the ability to exercise unwavering resolve and consistency, rendering it effortless for you to maintain your boundaries. Consequently, you will acquire authority and mastery over your Empathic ability, thereby liberating yourself from the perceived subjugation it may impose. Alternatively, you can exercise authority over the gift and employ it according to your requirements to sustain your life and fulfill your spiritual calling, while simultaneously cultivating a life of excellence.

Protect Your Energy Field

Shielding is a potent technique employed by individuals possessing empathic abilities in order to safeguard themselves against the influence of external energies. This is a method of establishing an energetic perimeter that can be maintained to ensure your sense of protection, alleviating the need for constant conscious effort. Initially, your energetic shield may necessitate ongoing deliberate strengthening. Once you acquire greater proficiency in this matter, nevertheless, it significantly simplifies the process.

A recommended protective measure to employ while venturing into public spaces or any environment where your abilities might be overly stimulated is commonly referred to as a "bubble shield." This protective shield is forged through the process of visualizing a luminous white glow emanating from your solar plexus. Subsequently, the illumination intensifies progressively, cleansing both your physical vessel and energy field while saturating them with a radiant white luminosity. Allow this illumination to gradually expand and manifest as a spherical energy field, encompassing a distance of four feet in every direction from your physical presence, encompassing even the lower depths of the Earth. This shield, once constructed, will remain fixed indefinitely, according to your wishes. Should you happen to perceive a state in which your defense is compromised or if, by any chance, you have inadvertently dismantled it, you may always restore it employing the identical approach. Certain individuals even opt to fabricate a fresh one each morning as a means to bolster their protection and stay safeguarded for the entirety of the day.

Whenever you sense a potential intrusion upon your energy, employ the technique of envisioning a protective shield, thereby fortifying it and preventing the entry of undesirable energies.

Draining Energy Individuals and Highly Sensitive Empathetic Individuals

Kaye is an empath. She possesses an exquisite inner essence that illuminates her environment. Not only does she possess the ability to perceive others' emotions, but she also assimilates them. When an individual experiences happiness, they are concurrently in a state of contentment. When an individual experiences sadness, it is also reflected within herself.

Glenda, her colleague, possesses exceptional physical attractiveness. She leads a comfortable existence, residing in a three-bedroom residence and owning two vehicles, caring for two children, all while being happily married to a commendable spouse. Nevertheless, she appears to lack the ability to fully comprehend the value of her possessions. She expresses dissatisfaction with every aspect of her life.

Kaye experiences a sense of physical frailty in close proximity to Glenda. It appears as though she is draining her vitality. She experiences a profound sense of exhaustion after engaging in conversation with her.

Glenda possesses a tendency to drain energy from others. She is beyond toxic. Nevertheless, can you provide a formal definition of an energy vampire? What is the reason behind their ability to deplete one's energy? How can one identify them?

Indeed, each interaction with another individual entails a reciprocal transfer of energy. Certain individuals, such as empaths, enrich us with positive energy, whereas others, such as energy vampires, deplete it.

Suppose, hypothetically speaking, that you have encountered an unfortunate circumstance of being dismissed from your employment, which has understandably resulted in a deep sense of anger and sadness permeating your emotional state. As a result, you chose to engage in a conversation with your mother on the matter. Your mother possesses a composed and affectionate disposition that instills a sense of tranquility within you. It gives you hope. It serves as an eye-opener that life is not inherently unfavorable.

Your mother possesses the characteristic of being an "energy-giver." She possesses a revitalizing impact. She instills a sense of safety and reassurance within you.

Now, supposing that you were to encounter a situation where you became unemployed, and subsequently resolved to engage in a conversation with your father. He does not exhibit the same level of warmth as your mother does. He possesses a discerning and exacting nature when it comes to critique. Following the disclosure of your issue, he proceeded to make derogatory statements such as "the likelihood of securing alternative employment is dim given your perceived lack of intellect" and "it is unsurprising that you encounter difficulties, given your perceived lack of worth or ability." In this particular situation, your father could be categorized as an individual who exhibits the characteristics of an energy vampire.

Energy vampires are individuals who exhibit emotional immaturity and possess a distorted perception that the world orbits solely around their being. Due to their insufficiently developed internal mental state, they rely on the emotional and psychic energy of others.

They occasionally exhibit an excessive inclination towards dramatic behavior. They partake in unpredictable conduct. Some energy vampires are just plain pessimistic. A number of them exhibit a propensity for severe criticism. Nevertheless, a subset of these individuals possesses a high level of threat, including individuals classified as sociopaths, narcissists, and even psychopaths.

Below are the typical traits exhibited by individuals who are toxic:

You experience a sense of sickness and fatigue upon engaging in conversation with them.

Engaging in conversation with energy vampires proves to be challenging. They engage in constant complaints and unwavering critique of everything you articulate. They evoke a sense of intellectual inadequacy.

Following an interaction with a toxic individual, one may experience a sensation of heaviness upon their shoulders. It is akin to navigating with the weight of two sacks of rice or two hollow blocks.

They extinguish the flame of your aspirations and ambitions.

During her youth, Eleanor aspired to pursue a career in ballet. Nevertheless, she hailed from a disadvantaged socioeconomic background, which rendered her parents unable to afford the expenses associated with enrolling her in ballet classes. According to her mother, dancing is considered a leisure pursuit rather than a vocation. Consequently, she made the decision to pursue a career in teaching.

Despite her competence in her profession, Eleanor harbored resentment as she fell short of realizing her childhood aspirations.

Rather than motivating her students, she undermines their aspirations. She imparts to her students that their physical appearance may not align with societal standards for success in the realm of celebrity, or that their intellectual capabilities may not meet the requirements typically associated with a successful career as an entrepreneur. She would generate an excess of one million justifications for why her students are unable to pursue their desired endeavors.

It may come as a surprise to you that there exists a considerable number of teachers whose thoughts and actions mirror those of Eleanor. Nevertheless, individuals with a negative and detrimental attitude can be encountered not only within educational institutions. They can be found in numerous locations. They have the potential to fulfill roles such as being your sibling, companion, colleague, life partner, or even your guardians.

They express statements such as:

Do you possess substantial expertise in this field?

I am uncertain about the viability of that approach.

It has already been completed previously.

"It's unproven."

I am uncertain whether someone would be willing to make a payment for it.

That appears to be a potentially hazardous situation.

It is anticipated that this task will pose considerable challenges.

The majority of individuals who express opposition or doubt have not accomplished their personal objectives and aspirations. Their existence lacks inspiration. They are veiled in feelings of self-disgust, envy, and apprehension, As a result, they project these anxieties onto other individuals.

They foster pessimistic perceptions regarding one's personal circumstances.

Toxic individuals possess the capacity to elicit adverse emotional responses and cultivate a pervasive feeling of discontent in an individual's existence. They instill within you a feeling of insufficiency. They utilize a passive-aggressive attitude to cultivate a feeling of being trapped, wherein individuals experience a continuous sense of obligation towards their work or difficulties without any respite.

Their exclusive focus is directed towards you solely when they are in need of your assistance or favors.

Each individual among us harbors that singular associate who solely makes contact with us in times of need. Toxic individuals direct their attention towards you only when it serves their own interests. They will leverage your resources and exhaust all that you own, ultimately leaving you devoid of any possessions.

Cultivating trust in one's intuition rests on possessing a sufficient level of self-assurance. Confidence encompasses the ability to effectively navigate and overcome challenges, as well as the determination to pursue opportunities that contribute to personal growth and improvement. Developing and enhancing one's confidence may require a certain amount of time before proficiently executing certain tasks. That is acceptable; however, it is imperative to approach the task with patience and treat yourself with compassion in the event of any setbacks.

Once you have enhanced your self-assurance, you can place greater reliance on your intuition in any scenario that may arise. Nevertheless, it is impossible to quantify intuition or ascertain its correctness in real-time, as previously established. Please bear in mind that this essence resides within your being, as it is inherent to your intuition and instincts.

Presented herein are several approaches that can facilitate the utilization of sound intuition while discerning people's behaviors.

1. Take a moment to decelerate and cultivate a state of mental clarity.

If given the opportunity, kindly allocate a moment to detach oneself from the present circumstances. Engage in self-reflection on the recent events. Attempt to articulate the impressions conveyed by your intuitive sense to yourself. It is possible that there are extraneous thoughts that are occupying your mind. Allocating a brief moment to introspect and engage in self-reflection will afford you the opportunity to streamline your cognitive faculties and discern your emotional state.

2. Take note of bodily sensations.

This aligns with the principle of cultivating mindfulness. In order to ascertain your emotional state in specific scenarios, it is imperative that you engage in somatic awareness and observe the physiological responses occurring within your body. You will commence the acquisition of the capacity to assign emotion labels that correspond to specific physiological conditions.

### 3. Focus on yourself.

It is conceivable that other individuals may hold divergent viewpoints regarding the individual or situation under contemplation. Certain individuals have gained your trust, while others have not. Regardless, it is crucial that you prioritize what holds significance to you and what appears genuine and pertinent in that given moment. Do not permit others to deceive you into disregarding the validity of your intuition. This will require fortitude and self-control. On certain occasions, it holds significance to acknowledge that you are adopting the viewpoints of others instead of crafting your own.

Positive psychology provides us with a structure through which we can actively pursue these objectives in life. Positive psychology provides a means of acquiring the essential aspects that we profoundly yearn for. Positive thinking is among the means through which these objectives can be accomplished.

A positive mindset significantly contributes to the enhancement of self-assurance and inner tranquility, regardless of the endeavor at hand. Positive thinking enables individuals to perceive the world through a more favorable lens, engage with challenging individuals from an improved standpoint, navigate the process of mourning with comparative smoothness, and essentially lead a healthy and optimistic existence. We all possess diverse strategies for cultivating a mindset of optimism; however, there is one undeniably consistent aspect. It is indispensable for our daily existence. As previously stated, there exists a profound and interconnected relationship between our mental processes and bodily functions. Concurrently, our physical state exerts a profound influence on our cognitive processes and emotional experiences. Please keep in mind that your thoughts shape your identity.

On the contrary, fostering pessimistic thoughts predisposes one to emulate what one despises, fail to meet personal standards, and impede the maintenance of a balanced state of being. Persistent negative thinking is often the cause of one's own decline and the decline of those around them. Consequently, due to this underlying factor, you persistently envision and anticipate circumstances in a pessimistic manner, perpetuating the ongoing cycle. Its embodied manifestation encompasses stress, muscular tension, and even compromised immune functionality. Furthermore, it can be argued that engaging in negative thinking can be considered a manifestation of harboring self-disdain to a certain degree. One becomes aware of negative aspects of one's own persona and inadvertently perpetuates such thoughts through one's behavior. Should you hold the belief that you do not possess physical attractiveness, it may be prudent for you to discontinue any endeavors aimed at enhancing your physical appearance or the manner in which you present yourself to society. You begin to perceive yourself as embodying the most negative aspects of your character.

Having expressed that notion, it is imperative to exercise dominion over, if not eradicate entirely, pessimistic thought processes. In addition, it not only has an impact on your overall welfare, but it also influences the individuals in your immediate surroundings, your professional endeavors, and the perception others have of you. In the end, a pessimistic mindset impedes one's ability to derive pleasure from life. It is crucial for you to cultivate a positive mindset in order to enhance not only your overall attitude towards society, but also your emotional well-being, mental equilibrium, and physical well-being.

# Typical People With High Emotional Intelligence

Given that personalities vary significantly from one person to another, the manner in which intelligence is developed is contingent upon the unique attributes of each individual. In the context of a regulated professional setting, it is noteworthy to observe the prevalent tendencies exhibited by individuals possessing remarkable cognitive prowess. The ensuing list illuminates a few widely recognized instances of such behavioral patterns.

● They have the capacity to articulate their thoughts and opinions in a tactful and unbiased manner, devoid of any apprehension regarding the possibility of causing offense to others.

● Frequently, they exhibit resilience in response to the introduction of new initiatives, despite any disagreement they may have with them.

- They consistently demonstrate a high degree of adaptability

They enjoy socializing with their colleagues outside of office hours.

- The individuals are granted the liberty to express their creativity, which is highly valued.

- They frequently engage in active listening during meetings and make valuable contributions based on their insights.

They consistently lend an empathetic ear to the troubles of others, demonstrating compassion towards them.

Leadership greatly benefits from possessing high emotional intelligence. Leaders with high emotional intelligence possess the ability to assemble a collective group of individuals who are profoundly interconnected and engaged in pursuing a shared vision. They frequently prioritize the quality and meaningfulness of their work over mere completion for the purpose of task accomplishment. A leader possessing elevated emotional intelligence can effectively inspire and enable their subordinates, while also adeptly navigating intricate and challenging decisions and displaying exemplary emotional acuity.

Possessing elevated emotional intelligence does not imply that an individual is continually joyful or situated in a positive state of mind. Essentially, this implies that the individual possesses the capacity to exercise sound judgment in navigating challenging circumstances, enabling them to make prudent choices. They possess the capacity to engage in emotional processing as a means of making rational decisions free from the influence of their emotions.

Illustrations of individuals with a deficient capacity for emotional intelligence.

Similar to the valued attribute of high emotional intelligence in professional and personal contexts, low intelligence plays a substantial role in shaping our interpersonal interactions. Individuals who possess inadequate emotional intelligence, including members of one's family, friends, employers, and colleagues, contribute significantly to the heightened tension and challenges experienced in numerous social encounters. In the majority of instances, it is plausible that one's personal emotional intelligence necessitates improvement.

To facilitate a deeper comprehension and determination of one's emotional quotient deficiency, presented below are nine prevalent indicators:

Getting into frequent arguments.

It is highly likely that individuals have encountered at least one person in their lifetime who habitually engages in arguments with others. Individuals you encounter in your life, including acquaintances, kin, or occasionally unfamiliar individuals, may engage in disagreements with these particular individuals. This can be attributed to the fact that individuals with low emotional intelligence encounter difficulties in perceiving and comprehending the emotions of others, often engaging in arguments without taking into account the possible emotional state of the other person involved.

Lack of empathy or the incapacity to discern the emotions of others.

Individuals exhibiting low Emotional Intelligence often display a pronounced lack of awareness pertaining to the emotions and sentiments of others. As an illustration, they encounter difficulty comprehending the reasons behind their friends' displeasure or their co-workers' irritation. Furthermore, they frequently experience a sense of obligation to become irritated with others due to the expectations placed on them to empathize with and comprehend the emotions of others. While this assertion remains valid for individuals possessing a high level of Emotional Intelligence (EI), those with lower levels of EI exhibit a deficiency in accurately appraising the emotions of others. The mere subject of emotions often elicits a strong sense of frustration among individuals with a low level of emotional intelligence.

Believing that others exhibit an undue level of emotional responsiveness.

Individuals with diminished emotional intelligence may exhibit a proclivity for making jests during inopportune instances. For instance, they may choose to employ humor immediately following a funeral or a grievous occurrence. When individuals fail to elicit the desired response to their ill-timed humor, individuals with low emotional intelligence might perceive others as overly sensitive. They encounter difficulty comprehending and interpreting the emotions of others, consequently experiencing challenges in perceiving the emotional context within specific circumstances.

Ignoring or disregarding the perspectives of others.

Individuals with low emotional intelligence often exhibit a tendency to possess an unwavering belief in their own correctness, vehemently defending their position while adamantly refusing to consider alternative perspectives or opinions. These individuals commonly exhibit a tendency towards pessimism and demonstrate a pronounced inclination for critically scrutinizing the emotions of others.

Attributing fault to others when circumstances do not unfold as expected.

Individuals with diminished emotional intelligence lack a comprehensive comprehension of their own emotions and their proclivity to give rise to adversities. In situations where circumstances do not unfold favorably, their primary response is to attribute responsibility to individuals in their vicinity. Frequently, they tend to attribute responsibility to the fundamental nature of the situation or the behaviors of others. A frequently employed counterargument that these individuals utilize is that they were left with no alternative course of action, and that it is the lack of understanding displayed by others regarding their prevailing circumstances. They have a tendency to adopt a victim mentality as a means of evading accountability.

Ineffectiveness in managing situations fueled by emotional intensity.

In situations where intense emotions emerge, individuals with low emotional intelligence encounter difficulties in understanding and making sense of these emotions. They have a tendency to seek escape from such situations in order to evade the need to confront them. Furthermore, it is highly prevalent for these individuals to conceal their emotions and sentiments from others.

Sudden Emotional Explosions.

As evidenced by the given instances of high emotional intelligence, a key factor lies in an individual's aptitude to effectively manage and modulate their emotions. Individuals who grapple with emotional intelligence encounter difficulties comprehending their own emotions and subsequently regulating them. They frequently exhibit unforeseen and seemingly unmanageable emotional outbursts.

Maintaining friendships is difficult.

Individuals with diminished emotional intelligence frequently exhibit a lack of sensitivity and convey themselves in a manner that is harsh and confrontational. Consequently, they encounter challenges in establishing meaningful friendships and building rapport with others. Given that friendship necessitates mutual reciprocity, individuals with low Emotional Intelligence encounter challenges in maintaining friendships. Additionally, they struggle with various aspects integral to friendship, such as the exchange of emotions, provision of emotional support, and demonstration of compassion.

Lack of empathy.

Given that individuals with diminished emotional intelligence struggle to comprehend the emotional states of others, they frequently experience difficulty in demonstrating empathy towards others. They possess a fundamental inability to comprehend the emotions experienced by others, thereby greatly inhibiting their capacity to adopt their standpoint, let alone exhibit empathy.

## 6 - Determine an Inception Date for Accomplishment

According to Parkinson's Law, work tends to increase in duration to occupy the entirety of the allotted time for its completion. When we allocate more time to accomplish a task or goal, it consequently takes us a longer period to achieve it. Hence, it is imperative that we acquire the knowledge of effectively employing Parkinson's Law to our benefit by establishing more concise timeframes within which to accomplish the objective or task.

## 7 - Determine and Address All Potential Obstacles and Hindrances

Recognizing obstacles should not deter you but rather assist you in preventing any unforeseen setbacks that may arise, enabling you to formulate the most efficient strategies feasible. By acknowledging the challenges at hand, one's mind should subsequently engage in contemplation of potential remedies to resolve these foreseeable circumstances.

## 8 - Establish Your Key Performance Indicators

An illustration of a pivotal indicator is the quantity of outbound solicitation calls you will undertake. Once the primary indicator has been determined, you establish an objective for that specific key indicator.

The purpose of this step is to assist you in determining the crucial tasks that must be completed daily, which will contribute significantly to the achievement of your overall objective. By prioritizing and fully committing to completing a task before moving on, one can effectively reduce the time spent on that task by approximately 80% compared to attempting to accomplish the same task in smaller increments.

## 9 - Develop a strategic course of action

Attempting to achieve an objective without a strategic framework is akin to endeavoring to construct a high-rise building without prior thorough planning and meticulous blueprint creation. The absence of blueprints will result in a sluggish, vexing, and remarkably costly construction procedure.

The aforementioned principle is equally applicable to your objective; if you neglect the process of strategizing, achieving your goal will be tedious, vexing, and costly. The expense may not always be in terms of financial value, but rather in terms of wasted time, strained relationships, etc. Devise strategic arrangements to embark on manifesting the envisioned future without delay.

## 10 - Demonstrate effective organization skills

In ordertoexercise control overone'sownexistence, it isessentialto maintain a propersenseof order. Furthermore, toachieveanauthenticstateoforganization, one mustimplementtheprinciplesof organization in everyaspectofone's life. If your physical environment is disorderly, the same will be true for your mental state.

Ensure that your workspace is immaculate when you engage in planning or executing a task. If you encounter any documents for which you are unable to take immediate action, please place them temporarily on the floor and proceed with your tasks.

11 - Employ the principle of leverage

Leverage refers to the capacity to exert minimal effort in order to attain maximum accomplishment. One instance of this can be seen as "OPK," which refers to the information possessed by individuals besides oneself. An excellent approach to harnessing leverage is to actively seek out a mentor. By engaging in this practice, you can efficiently allocate your resources by bypassing the experimental phase and promptly realizing the desired outcomes, leading to time and cost savings.

Through the establishment of a mastermind group, you are able to leverage the collective knowledge, resources, and networks of several other individuals, thereby expanding your reach to a greater number of potential collaborators who could assist you in achieving your objectives.

## 12 - Cultivate Self-motivation for the Development of Discipline

Consider the justifications for achieving your objective rather than creating excuses for not pursuing them. As one engages in the tasks that might be disliked, yet contribute to bringing oneself closer to the desired objective, a heightened sense of gratification, achievement, and tranquility is likely to be experienced.

There will be challenges in maintaining forward momentum, particularly if you do not observe immediate outcomes. Nonetheless, persevere nonetheless. One feasible method for accomplishing this objective is to consistently remind oneself of the underlying motivations driving the pursuit of one's goal, while also continuously maintaining focus on the ultimate outcome.

13 - Responsibility and answerability

Hence, the involvement in a mastermind group can prove highly advantageous as it provides us with a reliable individual to whom we can furnish progress updates. This person not only fosters our advancement but also ensures that we are held responsible for completing the remaining tasks associated with our goals and related benchmarks. Please bear in mind that increased levels of accountability will lead to more significant and favorable outcomes.

Fourteen - The practice of auto-suggestion

Autosuggestion entails the process through which an individual imparts instructions or internally organizes the subconscious mind, typically with the intent of cultivating a particular belief or systematically structuring one's mental associations. One method of employing autosuggestion is to record a few affirmative assertions like "I generate an annual income of $100,000" onto an index card, which you should consistently keep with you.

When the occasion arises, particularly in the morning upon waking or before going to sleep, even during breaks at work, it is advisable to commence the recitation of the written content on the card with utmost conviction and an inner assurance that what is being articulated (as per the written information on the card) about oneself is undeniably accurate.

We recommend maintaining a positive tone for the statements and employing the present tense, as the subconscious mind predominantly processes information through visual imagery. For instance, if one were to state, 'I am debt-free,' the subconscious mind would solely perceive the word 'debt' and consequently direct its attention towards acquiring more of it. A positive and present tense autosuggestion to express this idea formally could be, 'I am financially independent' or 'Money effortlessly flows towards me.'

Exhibiting Inherent Responsibility

Personal responsibility not only mirrors, but also engenders self-assurance. Individuals possessing an elevated sense of self-assurance perceive themselves as being accountable for the outcomes and events in their lives. They possess a sense of structure and self-sufficiency. They willingly accept responsibility for their opinions, actions, and livelihoods. It also entails assuming accountability for the outcomes of your decisions and actions, encompassing both favorable and unfavorable consequences, rather than attributing blame to oneself or others. It necessitates a sense of yearning to examine and glean insights from one's mistakes in order to seek solutions and progress.

In juxtaposition to young females, during the period of adolescence, young males tend to display attentiveness and assertiveness, thereby enabling their autonomy. The self-assurance of young females begins to suffer from the age of nine, and by the onset of puberty, they lag behind. Sensations of frailty and the need for external validation, particularly regarding one's physical appearance, escalate as self-assurance diminishes. Although it tends to be observed that young men exhibit more professional experimentation than young women, it is important to recognize that if young women are discouraged from taking risks or pursuing goals, they may develop a mentality of inadequacy instead of capability. Consequently, over time, such young women may develop a distorted outlook on life. The lack of workplace comradery and trust can ultimately result in a state of despondency.

The establishment of personal confidence necessitates taking responsibility for one's unhappiness and problems. Subsequently, they would attain the capability of undergoing alteration. A comprehensive analysis revealed that individuals who won the lottery ultimately reverted back to their initial state of affluence. Securing a lottery victory or encountering the ideal life partner merely imparts transitory contentment. Ultimately, our sense of well-being is determined by our confidence, deliberations, and actions.

Assuming responsibility can be agonizing when there is a lack of confidence. Individuals, on the other hand, resort to rationalization and casting blame on others, compelled by their heightened emotional distress. This behavior is truly bothersome to those in their vicinity, and it hampers their ability to interact with others.

Sandy consistently exhibited a tendency to delay tasks and submit her work past the designated deadline, accompanied by a multitude of justifications, thus causing annoyance to her manager.

Upon being criticized, she harbored strong animosity towards her supervisor, alleging blame towards him, as her own self-disdain grew. Through encouraging her to take responsibility for her behavior and delving into her fears and introspection that nurtured her spirit, she was able to alter her behavior. She developed a sense of self-worth and began to foster a positive self-image, which consequently gained her manager's confidence.

Self-esteem does not imply fault or blame; rather, it should prompt a thorough examination into the factors and circumstances that have shaped one's current life situation. Search for arrangements. Inquire about the underlying assumptions, beliefs, or mindsets that influenced your choices and behavior, and identify possible courses of action for the future.

Avoiding personal accountability positions you as a vulnerable individual relying on the change of others in order to attain a sense of comfort. That approach is not sustainable in the long run, as it is impossible to alter the nature of others, and even accommodating their desires temporarily only provides transient satisfaction. The additional remarkable experience of being in complete control of all the events in your life can also have a detrimental impact on your self-esteem. Engaging in self-blame for every mishap, ailment, and accident entails an unrealistic level of control assumption. Furthermore, you are not responsible for another individual's harmful behavior, but you are accountable for your own response to it. Instead of inquiring about the motive behind the person's actions, it is advisable to ask questions such as, "What are the beliefs that influence my ability to tolerate it?" "What boundaries do I establish?" "How can I enhance my own security?" "What are the potential consequences if I do not alter my response?"

Consider what remarkable outcomes could arise if you were to take responsibility for your happiness, financial stability, overall well-being, and physical health. What are the benefits of refraining from taking on responsibility for one's own well-being, finances, objectives, emotions, and relationships? It is highly probable that you find solace in contemplating your own being in areas where your self-awareness continues to grow. You experience a sense of achievement, bolstering your self-assurance. It will be diminished in the areas where you lack proficiency.

Mary complained about the series of men she encountered in her life who blatantly and financially took advantage of her. Instead of altering her behavior and choices, she sought solace in family and friends who shared the same closed-mindedness, thus perpetuating the pattern. Upon finally comprehending that there were no saviors forthcoming, she initiated her process of amelioration. She took responsibility for herself and realized her resilience. Due to a traumatic upbringing characterized by significant mistreatment during her early years, she had become convinced that she was incapable of attracting genuine affection from others. Reflecting on her past and confronting her grievances towards those responsible enabled her to escape an oppressive relationship and cease perpetuating intricate patterns in her interpersonal connections.

Individuals experience a growing sense of achievement when they take action, and those who are oriented towards proactive behavior tend to possess elevated levels of self-worth. They take action irrespective of their emotional state. They lack faith in the possibility of change and do not expect others to initiate transformation. While it is crucial to be aware of thoughts and emotions, allowing them to hinder proactive behavior can potentially undermine one's self-efficacy and, ultimately, their confidence. It is important to bear in mind that the realm of business necessitates thoughtful actions aimed at resolving a problem. This encompasses activities such as documenting, expressing sentiments, compiling a roster, gathering information, composing correspondence, pondering an issue, arriving at a declaration or decision, or even adjusting one's mindset.

Contemplate an area within your personal sphere where your level of self-assurance is lacking. How can one progressively take on more personal responsibility? What specific action could enhance one's sense of self-sufficiency and provide a sense of tranquility when reflecting on oneself?

Assuming responsibility for your self-assurance is vital for overcoming low self-esteem. That entails assuming ownership and accountability for one's own life. By failing to assume liability, you are undermining your own efforts. You have the tendency to subconsciously undermine your confidence through your verbal expressions, thoughts, and behaviors that effectively shift responsibility onto others. It is possible that you do not comprehend it.

Regardless, you have the ability to make that alteration. Assuming responsibility for your conviction is imperative for making progress in your life.

## Because Of Your Food

I often experience a mild melancholy on Mondays and Tuesdays, as I typically endure the remnants of my indulgence from Saturday night. Moreover, my occupation in the public sector failed to elicit a sense of fulfillment. Typically, during Tuesday evenings, I partook in athletics, engaging in rigorous interval training that involved intense 100-400 meter sprints, leaving me utterly exhausted. This endeavor required significant effort, however, it would subsequently elicit a profound sense of satisfaction. Abruptly, a surge of vitality coursed through my being.

During another phase in my life, I was facing a period of adversity. I encountered difficulties in the realm of dating and experienced a degree of stress in my professional career. During my commute home, it was customary for me to make a brief stop at the nearby store to procure food supplies. However, it became a recurring occurrence that I would also take the opportunity to obtain vegan chocolate delicacies during these visits. This transient gratification, nonetheless, instilled in me a measure of unease and subsequently aggravated my state. The resurgence of pessimistic thoughts would inundate my mind, subsequently rekindling my distress.

Upon careful observation, I have discerned a certain recurring pattern and consequently decided to restrict my consumption to whole foods exclusively during weekdays. Furthermore, I have reinstated my fasting routine and resumed my gym regimen. That singular endeavor did not alleviate my troubles entirely, albeit it did contribute to an ameliorating effect as I recommenced prioritizing self-care.

When considering nutrition and exercise, we frequently direct our thoughts towards our physical aesthetics, postulating that adhering to a healthy diet and engaging in physical activity will enhance our physique, whereas neglecting these practices will result in a less desirable physical state. Based on my personal experiences and ongoing educational journey, I can confidently affirm the veracity of this statement. However, it is crucial to recognize that the implications stemming from nutrition and exercise extend far beyond our current understanding.

A significant literary work that I will make repeated allusions to, just as I did in my previous publication, is the renowned book and instructional offering titled 'Unstoppable' penned by the esteemed author, Ben Angel. A literary work that thoroughly delves into the intricate connection between dietary choices, physical activity, and their profound impact on one's physical well-being, mental state, and emotional equilibrium.

I strongly advocate for this specific course.

What relevance does this hold to one's sense of self-worth? Based on the narrative and my prior statements, it can be inferred that by nourishing one's body with substandard sustenance, an individual is essentially asserting their inherent worthiness of such provisions. By taking proper care of your physical well-being, you will experience heightened vitality, enhanced mental acuity, and an overall sense of self-satisfaction.

It is imperative to note that each individual may possess distinct sensitivities, preferences, and dietary needs. It is essential to seek out the optimal solution for oneself in order to experience a sense of well-being.

Regarding physical activity, it is worth noting that engaging in exercise stimulates the release of endorphins, a neurochemical that creates a positive sensation within the body. Physical activity does not necessarily need to entail engaging in a marathon-like regimen every day, nor does it require dedicating two entire hours per day; rather, it can encompass a duration of twenty to thirty minutes of exercise. Ideally, an activity that promotes perspiration. You are affirming your worth and value to yourself and your body. Engaging in self-care is an act of self-love and nurturing oneself.

A highly efficacious method to enhance your understanding of your dietary and physical fitness habits is through the practice of maintaining a journal. This leads me to the next step in your course of action...

Action:

Upon the conclusion of each day, retrieve your journal and initiate the process of composing two lists. One enumeration comprises the instances that elicited positive feelings within me today, and that I should strive to engage in more frequently. The alternative enumeration focuses on the occurrences that did not generate favorable emotions and deliberates on methods to eliminate them from my life.

Through deliberately selecting which exercise and nutrition activities elicit positive experiences, one will gradually discern between advantageous and disadvantageous behaviors. Acquiring knowledge of these matters and discerning appropriate courses of action will contribute to your well-being and consequently foster an enhanced sense of self-esteem.

## Managing Unfavorable Thoughts

Negative thoughts can be likened to the act of worrying and indulging in excessive contemplation, but the key distinction lies in the circumstance where one is simply harboring a state of unadulterated negativity. Certainly, it is understandable that you may have concerns; however, it is worth noting that the disparaging thoughts you internalize tend to dominate the majority of your mental space. Negative thinking and worrying possess a shared characteristic in that they both necessitate recognition. As previously mentioned in the preceding section, it is essential to avoid passively awaiting the resolution of these issues; one must actively address them by repelling them, diverting attention from them, or refraining from downplaying their significance. Why? Because they get worse. It resembles a bothersome sibling: They persistently prod you until you reach a breaking point or address their presence.

Could you please elaborate on your approach for managing negative thoughts? It is imperative that you recognize their presence and accord them due attention. Analyze them thoroughly and identify the underlying source from which they originate. The reality concerning avoidance is that regardless of the specific things one attempts to evade or the extent of their efforts to forestall certain outcomes, those things will either subside temporarily before resurfacing, or they will intensify and persist for longer durations. As an illustration, in the event that you affirm to yourself, "I shall not emulate 'so and so'," or "I shall never embody or undertake 'whatever'," subsequently employing all feasible measures to evade adopting the behaviors or executing the designated action, it is plausible that a situation may ultimately transpire without your conscious realization. Subsequently, you might find yourself engaging in the very action you vehemently declared you would abstain from, or assuming the behavior of an individual whom you adamantly proclaimed you would never emulate. Negative thoughts operate in this manner, therefore refrain from evading their presence.

To address negative thoughts more efficiently, it is advisable to cultivate a sense of awareness towards them. If the sentiment you hold is that of self-doubt, with the belief that your capabilities are insufficient and shall forever remain so, you simply need to acknowledge its presence. Please refrain from making subjective evaluations of this matter, as it is neither inherently negative nor positive. Please refrain from interrogating or attempting to establish parameters for it. Just watch it. After allocating a brief period to observe and acknowledge the presence of this unfavorable thought, proceed to delve into its depths. Therefore, examine the events unfolding in your life and the changes occurring within yourself. Perhaps the sentiment of inadequacy may be attributed to the experiences of impact from unsuccessful pursuits or the inability to obtain the desired employment position. Identify the underlying cause and counter it by stating, "While it is understandable to assume that I am not competent enough since I did not secure the desired job, it is essential to recognize that alternative prospects exist within the same professional domain." "If I desire to, I can perpetually engage in the examination of alternative avenues."

After carefully observing, pausing for reflection, identifying the underlying thought, and thoroughly investigating the rationale behind it, one should assess their emotions post-engagement in these practices. It is likely that you will experience increased productivity and potentially even an improvement in your overall well-being.

Redirect Your Attention Towards a Positive Aspect

By directing your attention towards humorous memes, seeking out light-hearted expressions, or engaging in conversations with individuals who exude positivity, you can effectively divert your focus from negative thoughts. This does not entail evading them, but rather redirecting your attention until a more opportune moment arises for their resolution. Direct your focus towards shifting your thoughts towards joyful memories or any other stimuli that evoke a smile.

Practice Self-Love

An individual in my proximity would often advise me, "Upon receiving one's remuneration for diligent labor, it is prudent to set aside or allocate an amount equivalent to 10%, or alternatively, utilize said portion for personal gratification." I heeded this counsel and gradually experienced an improvement in my overall well-being. Our preoccupation with tending to our financial obligations, such as bills, rent, and sustenance, or attending to the needs of others, often leads us to neglect our own well-being. Self-care involves extending the same level of compassion and consideration to oneself as one would generously offer to one's intimate circle of friends or beloved family members. In the event that your negative thoughts continue to endure, address them in a manner akin to how you might respond if an individual dear to you were conveying these thoughts to you.

Cease the pretense of placating your negativity.

It is possible that an avoidance response has been cultivated in an effort to prevent the occurrence of negative thoughts. When one's negative thoughts spontaneously arise or are elicited by external stimuli, they are identified as intrusive thoughts. One illustration of behavioral change pertaining to intrusive thoughts may manifest as follows:

If an individual encounters aggressive ideations in the presence of knives or while handling a knife, it is advisable for them to either eliminate knives from their vicinity or refrain from handling them altogether.

If individuals encounter intrusive thoughts involving children, they might consider restricting their engagement with them, exercising heightened caution in their gaze, and even actively avoiding scenarios involving tasks such as changing or bathing them.

Step 2: Understand your value

Were you aware that individuals who possess unwavering confidence frequently exhibit a pronounced ability to make clear and resolute decisions? A noteworthy aspect of successful individuals is their tendency to efficiently make minor decisions without undue delay. They refrain from engaging in excessive analysis. Their ability to make rapid decisions stems from their comprehensive understanding of the overarching goal and desired outcome.

However, is it possible to ascertain the specifics of your desires?

The initial step entails your undertaking the task of determining your values. As stated by acclaimed author Tony Robbins, there exist two pivotal categories of values: end values and means values. These two categories of values are associated with the desired emotional state, encompassing happiness, a sense of security, and fulfillment, among various other factors.

Means Values

These pertain to methods by which you can elicit the specific emotion you seek. Money, frequently functioning as a medium rather than a goal, provides a prominent illustration. It represents an opportunity for attaining financial autonomy, a desired aspiration that possesses intrinsic worth.

Ends Values

This pertains to sentiments sought after, such as love, joy, and a feeling of protection. They represent the offerings that align with the values inherent in your resources and capabilities. For example, the funds will provide you with a sense of assurance and fiscal welfare.

Put simply, the means value pertains to the aspirations one believes they must pursue in order to ultimately achieve the desired end values. It is crucial for you to attain a clear understanding of your values in order to facilitate quicker and well-informed decision-making. Consequently, this will instill within you a stable and unwavering sense of self, from which you derive enduring confidence. One must assert control over their life rather than allowing life to dictate their actions.

One method by which you can achieve this is by ensuring the explicit articulation of your ultimate objectives. To initiate the process, it is recommended that you allocate a minimum of one to two hours per week for the purpose of documenting your ultimate values. In order to reach that destination, commence by articulating the values which you aspire to refine in order to manifest your envisioned existence.

A list of inquiries that may aid in gaining a better understanding of the situation encompasses: "

What are some of the most significant aspects in your life?

Are there aspects that fail to evoke your concern within the scope of your existential journey?

In the event that you were confronted with a challenging decision, which principles would you adhere to and which ones would you overlook?

If you are a parent, what are some of the principles you intend to inculcate in your children?

Step three: Cultivate personal contentment

Opting for felicity is a deliberate decision, and the most formidable impediments often stem from internally imposed limitations, such as beliefs of being undeserving of joy.

If you do not perceive yourself as deserving of joy, it follows that you also lack the conviction that you are entitled to the positive aspects of life, the sources of happiness, and this very belief will hinder your ability to attain happiness.

You can be happier. It relies on the particular aspect you choose to concentrate on. Thus, choose happiness.

Happiness is not a passive result of external circumstances. It is an alternative, yet it requires exertion. Do not anticipate someone else to be the source of your happiness, as this may result in an indefinite period of waiting. Your happiness cannot be determined by any external factor or individual.

Happiness is an intrinsic emotional state. Only 10 percent of your happiness can be attributed to external circumstances. The remaining 90% encompasses your conduct and the mindset you choose to embrace when confronted with those circumstances. The formal rephrasing of the statement could be as follows: "The scientifically determined factors contributing to happiness consist of external conditions accounting for 10%, genetic predisposition making up 50%, and intentional activities, encompassing learning and experiential exercises, contributing 40% to overall well-being." There exists a natural variation in the innate happiness levels amongst individuals; nevertheless, those who are born less happy have the potential to achieve greater happiness through diligent engagement in the prescribed exercises compared to individuals with a higher natural propensity for joy who neglect such practices. A shared characteristic between both equations is the limited impact of external circumstances on our state of happiness.

Typically, we tend to presume that our circumstances exert a significantly more substantial influence on our overall state of happiness. An intriguing phenomenon unfolds wherein happiness often manifests itself when one ceases active pursuit of it. Savor every single moment. Anticipate the occurrence of extraordinary occurrences and promising prospects at every turn, and in due course, you will encounter them. The more attention you devote to something, the more likely you are to observe a greater quantity or frequency of it. Choose to prioritize opportunities, opt to direct your attention towards the positive, and elect to center your focus on cultivating happiness. Make your own happiness.

Relationships

Interpersonal connections encompass the dynamic interaction between two distinct individuals, each with their own unique personalities, diverse backgrounds, and varied personal histories. In instances where there exists a divergence, it becomes a source of intrigue, as there is an undeniable thrill in engaging and conversing with individuals who have encountered realities starkly contrasting to our own.

Now, while this disparity may indeed be unexpected, it also gives rise to discord, as your origins do not align. You did not undergo similar experiences; your upbringing did not entail the same notions and influences. Hence, in the context of being in a relationship, it is effortless to perceive it as a form of rivalry. Additionally, one can perceive it as a situation where one party emerges victorious while the other party experiences defeat.

Regrettably, individuals with diminished self-assurance tend to naturally incline toward adopting an approach in which they abstain from asserting their requirements and desires, out of apprehension that doing so might result in the departure of the other party. To clarify, it can be surmised that your relationship was overshadowed by the predominant fear of losing them. At that juncture, it ceases to be a relationship.

It is imperative to maintain awareness that relationships encompass a framework and establish conditions that facilitate growth for both individuals involved. It is challenging to make progress when one consistently denies oneself. It is challenging to fully flourish when one feels compelled to restrain oneself out of apprehension that the other individual in the relationship would be lost. In the end, the absence of self-assurance leads to the fusion of your individuality within the persona of your partner in the context of a relationship. In essence, the focal point of the link revolves around their individual requirements, aspirations, their forthcoming endeavors. Consequently, you find yourself compelled to offer various justifications for allowing such circumstances to unfold.

A frequent rationalization is to deceive oneself by falsely believing that one is making maximum efforts to sustain the relationship. You are refraining from discussing the link as you are ultimately not involved in the matter. The affiliation does not pertain to your significant other. Regrettably, this is the point at which your support manifests as self-denial, neglect of your own needs, and suppression of your individuality within the context of the relationship. Your sole endeavor appears to be providing assistance solely to your partner, neglecting others in the process.

It is imperative that you exhibit unwavering steadfastness in your commitment to persevere in the act of loving. You must establish and cultivate your own unique identity. It is imperative to ensure that your relationship is established upon a firm basis of mutual respect and egalitarianism. These abilities are unattainable in the absence of self-assurance.

In order for your relationship to foster a state of well-being, it is imperative to garner attention. The other party is required not only to acknowledge your presence but also to exhibit adequate respect towards you and consider your feedback. Moreover, they must occasionally yield to your authority. Put differently, it is necessary for you to make your presence heard. This task is nearly unattainable in the absence of self-assurance.

In addition, the presence of self-assurance contributes significantly to one's interpersonal dynamic. The reality is that the notion of a flawless relationship is entirely elusive. Individuals have the capability to make mistakes and, indeed, they often do. Either you or your partner may engage in acts of infidelity. One may utter inappropriate statements at inopportune moments, thereby inflicting harm upon one another. Numerous unforeseen circumstances could potentially arise.

In light of these circumstances, it is crucial to maintain perseverance. It is crucial to persevere and recover in a relationship. Without any doubt, it is possible that your partner may utter words that are extremely devastating, highly hurtful, and deeply humiliating, ultimately leading you to effortlessly surrender anddecide to walk away. However, you don\\\'t. If the relationship holds value, one would not engage in such behavior. You hang in there. It requires resilience. One must strive to endure and persist until the communication is established in a manner that facilitates the recipient's comprehension and subsequent growth from the aforementioned unfortunate incident, thereby earning the due reverence. That outcome is unlikely to occur unless you possess an adequate amount of self-assurance beforehand.

It is exceedingly effortless for your relationship to become exceptionally delicate due to a profound sense of inadequacy, to the extent that it is inevitable that one of you will eventually withdraw. If you deem this task challenging, it is important to comprehend that establishing a relationship necessitates a certain level of self-assurance. Why? It is imperative that you distinguish yourself from the rest of the contestants.

In the event that your significant other possesses considerable physical charm or allure, it is highly likely that they would attract the attention of multiple potential admirers. It is contingent upon the degree of their appeal. Naturally, the greater the charm or allure of a partner, the higher the level of competition one encounters. Nevertheless, even in the scenario where your partner may not possess significant physical appeal, it remains probable that there exists at least one individual who holds an interest in your partner, or alternatively, your partner themselves may exhibit an attraction towards another individual. In order to distinguish oneself from competitors, it is imperative to possess a sense of self-assurance. At minimum, it is crucial for you to present a compelling argument to justify why your potential partner should choose you over other candidates.

# Techniques For Mitigating Fears And Insecurities By Engaging In Immersive Real-Life Encounters.

Do you experience apprehension when confronted with situations involving a substantial gathering of individuals? Do you experience feelings of anxiety prior to engaging with unfamiliar individuals?

Understanding the Problem

Should this be the situation, it is imperative that you ascertain the cause. Additionally, it is imperative to pinpoint the precise elements of being in a social gathering and engaging with unfamiliar individuals that instill a sense of anxiety within you. There exists a discernible pattern in the gradual culmination of fear or anxiety. The initiation often commences with a stimulus for the majority of individuals. Apprehension could potentially arise upon learning that you are required to partake in the social gatherings. Certain individuals with introverted tendencies may develop a disliking for social gatherings if they were not anticipated. Some individuals experience a sense of apprehension when they are required to participate in a social event that draws attention to their presence. This apprehension is typically associated with one's social performance.

Fear is normal. It is an inherent mechanism of the human body to signal potential threat. Nevertheless, it has the potential to impede our social interactions, particularly when fear establishes a pattern of hindering our responsibilities.

Allow us to consider the case of Mike. Mike is on the verge of celebrating his third Christmas within the organization. He abstained from attending the initial two corporate Christmas parties due to the presence of activities that may cause him embarrassment. He makes repeated attempts to convince himself to participate in the activity, yet invariably, his fear emerges victorious. Over the course of the previous two years, he consistently opts to remain at his residence at the eleventh hour while concocting justifications for his inability to attend.

During the previous two holiday gatherings, Mike failed to comprehend the reasons behind his unwillingness to attend. Nevertheless, upon scrutinizing the fear pattern, he arrived at the realization that it was the act of performing amidst the multitude that induced his anxiety. He derived pleasure from the prospect of engaging in social activities with his colleagues, and he anticipates with eagerness the opportunity to converse with certain individuals. Nevertheless, each time the notion of presenting before his colleagues enters his thoughts, he experiences a sense of unease. He initiates a process of envisioning situations in which he experiences feelings of embarrassment.

By identifying the precise aspect of the social gathering that Mike dreads, he could potentially circumvent the participatory segment rather than altogether abstaining from attending the entirety of the occasion.

Triggers encompass cognitive processes related to social activities that elicit fear responses within one's psyche. Once the onset of fear occurs, individuals with social anxiety engage in a sequence of actions that result in the avoidance of specific social activities. In the realm of professional environments, the non-attendance of specific events and engagements might be construed as lacking in cooperation and collaboration.

In order to mitigate the hindrance posed by social anxiety and facilitate active engagement, it is imperative to ascertain the precise underlying factor contributing to your anxiety. Outlined below are a few of the conventional social engagements that evoke apprehension among individuals:

• Delivering a speech in public • Engaging in public speaking • Addressing an audience publicly • Presenting before an assembled crowd • Making oral presentations in a public setting

• Engaging in an activity within the presence of a large assembly.

• Subjecting to ridicule or derision

• Delivering presentations to individuals holding authoritative positions •

Conducting presentations in the presence of individuals in positions of authority • Giving presentations to individuals with influential roles • Speaking before an audience comprising individuals in positions of power • Addressing a group of distinguished individuals during a presentation

• Engaging in a romantic encounter or encountering someone of romantic interest

• Delivering a theatrical presentation

• Initiating an informal dialogue

In the majority of instances, a considerable number of individuals come to the realization that their greatest apprehensions hold little significance and can indeed be confronted. Nevertheless, some individuals with introverted tendencies may struggle to summon the necessary resolve to confront their fears, even when they recognize the lack of likelihood for the feared outcome to actually transpire. Below are several strategies that can be employed to mitigate the influence of fear on one's behavior:

Exercise cognitive control to effectively cope with your anxieties

Socially anxious individuals frequently employ specific cognitive patterns. The following are a few examples:

• Hypotheses and projections

Individuals who experience anxiety tend to hold the belief that various situations present constant possibilities for them to endure embarrassment. They formulate numerous presumptions that precipitate their apprehensions. They additionally forecast the manner in which events are anticipated to unfold.

For individuals grappling with social anxiety, this tendency becomes ingrained.

When one starts to engage in assumptions and anticipations of alarming circumstances, it indicates the necessity to divert one's attention from the prevailing fear. Individuals employ distinct coping mechanisms to deal with fear. If you happen to be present in the office during moments of fear, one viable approach would be diverting your focus towards work as a means of deterring its influence on your mindset.

• Pervasive pessimistic thinking

The suppositions and prognostications made by individuals of introverted disposition afflicted with social anxiety tend to be exacerbated by their profound pessimism. When contemplating these occurrences, their attention lies on the potential negative outcomes.

- Personalizing

When considering potential mishaps at social gatherings, individuals also consider the manner in which party attendees will respond to their actions. They hold the belief that individuals have the intention to ridicule them. They contemplate that their superiors are present with the intention of demeaning them.

- The physiological reaction known as the fight or flight response

Once fear sets in, stress hormones will subsequently trigger the activation of the fight or flight response. Socially anxious introverts tend to instinctively steer clear of the event. It is possible that they have opted not to participate in the occasion previously, and it appears that they fared well. Subsequently, when confronted with analogous forms of stress, they resolved to employ an identical coping mechanism.

Over the course of time, these cognitive frameworks acquire automatism as individuals encounter situations and activities that are unfamiliar to them. Persistent utilization of these cognitive and behavioral patterns hinders individuals from experiencing favorable outcomes and achievements in their social interactions.

It may be necessary for them to engage in activities that occupy and divert their attention on their mobile device, such as sending text messages to others. However, you are entitled to express your desire to genuinely connect with that individual. This individual must acquire a thorough understanding of empathy, as they currently lack the experience of authentically relating to others. They have become so accustomed to presenting themselves in a performative manner in their daily lives that they have lost touch with the experience of being carefree. They exhibit difficulties in fully engaging with the present situation. Occasionally, they believe they possess an adeptness for residing in the present, yet their actual ability to do so is lacking. They find themselves in a state of stagnation, feigning presence. They possess an extensive inventory of thoughts within their cognitive faculties, perpetually evaluating the ways in which they can facilitate a more convenient existence for themselves. They lack proficiency in performing tasks on behalf of others.

While this may not constitute the predominant attributes of an individual, they may occasionally exhibit such behavior, and that is deemed acceptable. It is permissible for an individual to conduct themselves in such a manner; one must simply acquire the ability to react in a suitable manner. Numerous individuals may enter into relationships with individuals perceived as social climbers due to their adeptness in articulating their desires and their ability to effortlessly initiate interpersonal connections. "They will experience a sense of disappointment as the social climber purposefully maintains a distance, cognizant of their tendency to exploit any opportunity that presents itself."

This individual exhibits a notable lack of empathy. It is highly likely that they had a protected upbringing during their childhood. Frequently, they encountered a lack of sufficient intellectual stimulation, or they received excessive praise regarding their exceptional qualities without proper consideration of the underlying reasons or methods behind their perceived specialness. It is crucial to provide a child with an explanation of why and in what manner they are unique. If one does not necessitate the cognitive process implicated in comprehending the rationale behind one's own significance, why would one presume one's own significance to be factual? This marks a significant divergence.

A prevalent issue encountered by numerous individuals, particularly among the elderly, pertains to the predicament of bias. They face greater challenges in developing empathy towards specific individuals due to their divergence from personal characteristics. They might possess unconscious or conscious prejudices towards individuals, assessing them based on physical or national attributes. This is an instance that clearly demonstrates a significant deficiency in empathetic qualities, as it is expected that an individual possesses the capacity to acknowledge the inherent humanity in others while simultaneously being mindful of their own being. Cultural context must be encompassed within the realm of empathy, and if one is unable to empathize with individuals who differ from them, they possess a deficiency in fostering empathy. If one possesses empathy solely towards individuals who share similar experiences, it becomes imperative to introspect and rectify this inclination, for it contradicts the fundamental essence of humanity. Empathy can be regarded as an embodiment of love; fundamentally, it can be viewed as synonymous with love.

Empathy can be experienced through the melodies of various cultural genres, as music serves as a universal language that resonates with individuals across diverse backgrounds. This also holds true for culinary experiences; they serve as fundamental means of connection we share with individuals from all corners of the globe. The following methods enable individuals to engage with alternative cultures and immerse themselves in unique experiences distinct from their own.

A framework was formulated to establish meaningful connections among individuals, irrespective of their variances. This phenomenon is commonly referred to as the collective consciousness, which undergoes continual modulation and expansion. We dwell within its boundaries; we are integral constituents of it. We have the ability to alter it. We can strive to establish a connection with it, and endeavor to deviate from it. The choice of action is within your purview, however, it shall endure. The collective unconscious can be perceived as a vast interplay of mental processes. We all have basic physiological needs such as nourishment, rest, and emotional connections, which represent only a fraction of the shared experiences we possess. As individuals, we possess a spiritual nature wherein our thoughts emanate vibrational energy that interconnects with the minds of others. One can experience this sensation by observing a specific city skyline or envisioning one's family or a serene waterfall. One can discern a palpable essence emanating from the photographer behind the lens, having experienced firsthand what you currently hold in your hands: a tangible representation crafted through their discerning eye and proficient utilization of a skillful instrument. It is conceivable to acknowledge that we, as human beings, are inherently interconnected and comprise a collective entity residing on this planet.

Does this statement appear to be meaningless? Well, then, it is. That is permissible; you may interpret it as nonsensical. However, once you gain a comprehensive comprehension of empathy, you will find that these words align with your understanding. You will have the opportunity to observe the interconnectedness of our shared atmosphere, the universal necessity of water consumption, and our mutual reliance on the sun. It is truly remarkable to recognize our inherent vulnerability and uncertainty, while still maintaining the capacity to extend love and support to one another throughout our shared experiences.

This represents the universal aspect of human existence known as "empathy," signifying that we are interconnected to some degree and that each individual is entitled to equal affection and security. We are collectively confronted with identical challenges, encompassing matters of existence and mortality, the unpredictable nature of life and assuredness, the realms of affection and creativity, as well as the realms of labor and finances. It is incumbent upon all of us to address this matter. And that millionaire? Indeed, it is highly likely that his apparent contentment may not truly reflect his inner state; it is worth remembering the age-old saying, "money cannot purchase happiness," as its validity remains unchanged even in present times.

## The Intersection of Anxiety and Psychological Well-being

Fear is constraining your progression due to its negative influence on your psychological well-being. Failure to actively seek new experiences and place oneself in unfamiliar circumstances may lead to a compounding of fear over time. The fear of the unknown may intensify as one develops an apprehension towards navigating novel situations, having consistently declined opportunities to engage with them for an extended period. For instance, should you have confined yourself solely within familiar bounds throughout the previous two years, you might currently harbor apprehension that should you ever choose to venture beyond those limits, you would experience such intense fear and uncertainty to the extent that you would be incapable of functioning adeptly. As a result, this tendency enables you to remain within your comfort zone for an extended duration, subsequently perpetuating the fear in question.

Chronic Fear

The experience of residing in a state of persistent apprehension may lead to the development of anxiety. Although it may not manifest as anxiety, maintaining a perpetual state of fear can give rise to numerous health-related concerns in the future. Several of these problems encompass gastrointestinal issues, compromised immune functioning, cognitive decline, and challenges in fear regulation over an extended period. Should your brain persistently experience fear, it shall inevitably affect your physical well-being, given that the physiological alterations induced by fear are intended to occur only momentarily. When the aforementioned changes endure in a consistent manner, due to the enduring presence of fear, it can adversely affect the physical well-being of the individual. In the event that you have experienced an intense sense of fear stemming from a daunting encounter, it is plausible that you recall feeling considerably fatigued subsequently. This can be attributed to the fact that fear exerts a considerable toll on the physiological well-being of individuals. A few of the physiological changes that it induces encompass augmenting the blood circulation towards muscles such as the lower extremities, suspending the digestive process, and dilating the pupils, among various other effects. These modifications collectively contribute to enhancing an individual's ability to engage in combat or flee; however, when they endure due to anxieties such as anticipatory fear, they no longer promote our well-being.

## The Correlation Between Fear and Levels of Self-Confidence and Self-Esteem

The correlation between fear and low self-confidence stems from a deficiency in self-assurance and a sense of unease in one's capacity to navigate unfamiliar circumstances. Should you find yourself lacking in self-assurance, it is probable that your confidence in your capabilities, particularly in terms of coping, is diminished. Each day, we are confronted with various challenges, and navigating novel and discomfiting circumstances is one such challenge that necessitates our ability to adapt and triumph. When experiencing a diminished sense of self-assurance, we lack confidence in our ability to effectively handle situations, which is directly correlated with the presence of fear. The experience of low self-esteem can manifest in various ways, such as the apprehension of incompetence, the concern of appearing foolish in the presence of unfamiliar individuals, or the unease of undergoing a psychological collapse.


When possessing elevated levels of self-esteem, we exhibit unwavering trust in our capacity to make sound decisions and seamlessly adjust to unfamiliar and challenging circumstances. We are capable of confronting unfamiliar circumstances elicits a sense of apprehension with the assurance that we possess the ability to overcome them, potentially deriving knowledge from the encounter. We refuse to succumb to fear and allow it to hinder us from embracing new endeavors that may evoke trepidation.

If our level of self-esteem is insufficient, it is probable that we will perceive ourselves as individuals of diminished worth or undeserving of certain opportunities. Additionally, this can give rise to apprehension as we may harbor concerns regarding potential rejection when interacting with unfamiliar individuals or navigating unfamiliar circumstances. Consider, for instance, a maiden encounter, wherein we would necessitate stepping beyond the realm of familiarity to rendezvous with a stranger, invest time acquainting ourselves with them, and ardently aspire for their delight in this shared venture. Individuals with a pronounced lack of self-confidence tend to anticipate unfavorable opinions of themselves, an absence of enjoyment during the date, and eventual rejection." This instills a sense of apprehension, which might potentially deter the individual from participating in a social outing such as a date. Consequently, there exists a strong correlation between self-esteem and fear.

In contrast, individuals possessing strong self-assurance would perceive themselves as generally likable, attributing any rejection of a second date to the other person's preferences or circumstances, rather than reflecting any personal inadequacy on their part. An individual characterized by elevated self-esteem possesses a strong sense of assurance in regards to their personality, behavior, and physical presentation. They might experience a certain level of anxiety on their first date, but they harbor no trepidation regarding potential rejection, as they possess a profound internal belief in their own self-worth that does not rely on external validation.

Fear arises when individuals with diminished self-assurance or self-regard encounter circumstances or encounters that may present them with perceived challenges. They lack the capacity to supersede these fear-induced emotions with cognitive reassurances of their competence, derived from their previous triumphs over daunting circumstances. The apprehension typically acts as a deterrent, dissuading them from venturing into such situations or encounters at their discretion, as their attention is fixated on the myriad of potential mishaps that might occur if they choose to expose themselves.

9 - Formulate strategies

Attempting to achieve a desired outcome without a well-structured strategy is akin to endeavoring to construct a towering skyscraper without first meticulously outlining the architectural plans. Absence of blueprints in the construction process may result in a decelerated, vexing, and exorbitant endeavor.

The aforementioned principle applies to your objective as well; if you neglect the opportunity to formulate strategies, the achievement of your goal will be hindered by delays, vexation, and financial burden. The expense may not always manifest in monetary terms, but rather in wasted time, strained relationships, and so on. Formulate strategies to initiate the construction of the desired future at this moment.

## 10 - Maintain a high level of organization

To exercise full control over one's life, it is imperative to maintain a sense of organization. True organization necessitates comprehensive and meticulous structuring in all facets of one's existence. If your physical environment is disorganized, then your mental state will also reflect the same disorder.

Please ensure that your workspace is immaculate before you begin the process of planning or undertaking a task. If there are documents that are beyond your control, temporarily place them on the floor and proceed with your tasks.

11 - Utilize the principle of leverage

Leverage refers to the capacity to exert minimal effort in order to achieve maximum results. One illustration of this is the acronym "OPK," which refers to the knowledge possessed by individuals other than oneself. One of the most effective methods to employ leverage is to actively seek out a mentor. By engaging in this practice, you can optimize your resource allocation by eliminating the iterative process commonly associated with trial and error, and instead expedite the attainment of desired outcomes.

By establishing a mastermind collective, you effectively harness the collective intellectual capital, resources, and networks of others, thereby expanding your reach to a larger audience that possesses the potential to aid you in achieving your objectives.

## 12 - Cultivate Self-Motivation to Foster Discipline

Consider the justifications for achieving your objective rather than finding excuses to neglect them. As you engage in the tasks that you find unpleasant yet propel you towards your objective, you will experience heightened satisfaction, achievement, and tranquility in your existence.

There may be instances where maintaining momentum poses challenges, particularly when immediate results are not apparent. Nevertheless, it is important to persist and persevere. One effective method would be to consistently reinforce your motivations behind achieving your objective and consistently maintain a focus on the ultimate outcome.

## 13 - Responsibility

This is why participating in a mastermind group can be highly advantageous; it provides us with a person to report to who will not just support our progress, but also ensure that we are held responsible for the tasks still outstanding in attaining our goals and associated indicators. Keep in mind that increased accountability leads to enhanced outcomes.

## 14 - The concept of autosuggestion

Autosuggestion involves the deliberate training of the subconscious mind to embrace a particular belief or to meticulously structure one's own mental associations, typically with a predetermined objective in mind. One method for employing autosuggestion is to document a set of affirmations, such as, "I generate an annual income of $100,000," on an index card, and ensure that card is consistently carried.

At any given occasion, whether it be at the start of each morning, prior to retiring for the night, during a work break, and so forth, initiate the practice of reciting the contents inscribed on the card with utmost conviction and an internal assurance that the statements written about oneself are indeed factual.

Maintain a positive stance and utilize the present tense while formulating statements, as the subconscious mind comprehends information through visual imagery. For example, if one were to state, 'I am debt-free,' the subconscious mind would only register the word 'debt,' therefore directing its focus on acquiring more debt. A positive, present tense autosuggestion for this concept could be, 'I am financially independent' or 'Money flows to me effortlessly.'

## Fifteen - Proceed with Action

Frequently, we assert that we will achieve our lifelong aspirations once we have accomplished certain ancillary objectives. Please bear in mind that there is no opportune moment quite like the present to undertake any endeavor, regardless of its nature. The United States did not achieve its independence by patiently anticipating the opportune moment, and likewise, neither shall you. Why not commence today on embarking toward improving the quality of life for yourself and your beloved ones?

\\\"Self-Pardon\\\"

In order to achieve personal liberation and perpetual growth in a state of boundless self-acceptance, it is imperative that we cultivate a mentality of "self-forgiveness" for our wrongdoings, irrespective of its groundedness in reality. Ultimately, we may arrive at the realization that there is no need for forgiveness. Despite deviating from our previous convictions, it can be argued that we were consistently innocent. We consistently strived to perform optimally, considering the inherent limitations imposed upon us, the persuasiveness of our desires and emotions at that moment, and the standards we subscribed to in that era.

The factor that ultimately determines risky behavior is closely linked to conventional psychological safeguards. Furthermore, it borders on the callousness for us to indict ourselves or regard ourselves with contempt for engaging in behaviors that, at the moment, we believed were necessary to protect ourselves from anxiety, shame, or emotional distress predominantly.

Nevertheless, it reflects a fundamental aspect of our predisposition and must be effectively integrated in order for us to fully develop. Until we come to recognize - or impose upon ourselves in some manner - fragmented aspects of our identity, complete and constrained self-awareness will consistently elude us in an ongoing manner.

Once we are prepared to diligently grasp the origins of these dull, inert elements within us, any self-evaluation associated with them begins to evoke a sense of severity and disgrace. Indeed, it is true that every individual possesses prohibited (and potentially irrational) desires and aspirations, irrespective of whether they encompass inflicting harm upon someone deemed objectionable, exerting unchecked authority over others, or engaging in public nudity. Once we reach a state of readiness to comprehend this concept, we find ourselves progressing significantly in embracing our true selves unconditionally. Recognizing the fact that, no matter how uncommon or regrettable, the overwhelming majority of our negative thoughts and fantasies likely involve minimal projections of insults, damages, or hardships from our past experiences, we can now reinterpret our deviations as being rather ordinary.

Moreover, as we gradually recognize and accept our inherent flaws, we can exert deliberate control over the manner in which these aspects of ourselves are expressed - specifically, in ways that ensure both our own well-being and that of others. As long as we have had the opportunity to reconnect with our innermost, authentic self, we will be approaching situations from a standpoint characterized by fondness and attentiveness. Hence, it is not within our nature to engage in any actions that would undermine our inherent disposition towards compassion and identification with all of humanity. The experience of possessing and integrating our various facets is truly remarkable. Additionally, as we cease to perceive ourselves as distinct entities but rather as interconnected beings, any perverse justification for causing harm to others disappears.

At this point, it should be apparent that self-acknowledgment bears no relevance to the pursuit of self-improvement in this particular regard. It does not entail rectifying any aspect within ourselves. By acknowledging ourselves, without passing judgment, we are essentially attesting to our identity, embracing both our strengths and weaknesses present in that moment.

The problem inherent in placing importance on individual growth is that such an orientation inevitably constrains self-recognition. Moreover, the attainment of true security and confidence is elusive as long as our self-esteem is predicated on our consistent self-improvement. Self-acknowledgment is contingent upon the present moment, rather than being contingent upon future arrangements, such as the notion of "I will be fine when..." . ".\\\" or \\\"Upon attaining . . . I will be fine. Self-acknowledgment entails being emotionally stable and content, regardless of any limitations or abilities. We do not disregard or reject our shortcomings or weaknesses; rather, we perceive them as inconsequential to our fundamental acceptability.

Finally, it is solely our own selves who establish the standards for our self-recognition. Moreover, in the event that we opt to cease self-assessment or self-monitoring, we can adopt a mindset of non-judgmental forgiveness. In fact, if we refrain from perpetuating our ingrained inclination to constantly critique and scrutinize ourselves, and instead make an effort to empathetically understand our past behaviors, we will come to realize that there is in fact no need for self-reproach (as the saying goes, "Tout comprendre..."). Certainly, we can offer assurance that there will be room for improvement in the future. In addition, it is important for us to candidly recognize our current shortcomings without disregarding them.

And yet, I find it challenging to uphold the notion that it is conceivable to acknowledge and appreciate ourselves while remaining committed to a lifelong pursuit of self-improvement. Embracing ourselves as we are does not imply that we will lack the motivation to pursue improvements or enhancements that make us increasingly effective, or that will promote the betterment of our own lives and the lives of others. It is fundamentally understood that self-acknowledgment bears no relation to these alterations. We need not necessarily seek to fortify our self-acknowledgment in a vigorous manner; rather, we simply must alter our perception of ourselves. Therefore, it appears that altering our procedures is solely dependent on personal preference rather than necessary for enhancing one's overall dignity.

It pertains to originating from a markedly distinct location. If the act of recognizing our own abilities and worth is contingent upon achieving it through hard work and maintaining strict discipline, then it remains perpetually vulnerable to risk. The perpetual endeavor of embracing and acknowledging our true selves can never be concluded. Even achieving the highest grade in any pursuit we undertake provides only a fleeting respite from our endeavors. The notion we are conveying to ourselves is that our worth is solely determined by our most recent achievement. We are unable to attain a state of self-recognition as we have inadvertently perceived our pursuit for such recognition as perpetual.

By adhering to such stringent standards, however, we unintentionally validate the manner in which our own caring guardians raised us. Nevertheless, we are undeniably neglecting ourselves - or failing to treat ourselves with the conscientiousness and consideration that our parents failed to provide for us.

In conclusion, it is only when we are fully prepared to wholeheartedly embrace ourselves, by fostering greater self-compassion and placing significant emphasis on our strengths rather than weaknesses, that we can ultimately absolve ourselves of our shortcomings and relinquish our desire for validation from others. Undoubtedly, we have made mistakes. However, this is true for every individual. The connection between our mistake and our personality is not valid (as it would imply an unfortunate case of misidentification!).

External Validation

I entered the workplace that morning as I had done on any typical day. I felt ok. I recently held a meeting with my manager during which I received commendation for my diligent execution of certain tasks. I experienced a sense of excitement and satisfaction with my accomplishments. I experienced a sense of significance and a feeling of being a valuable contributor to the organizational environment.

I perceived myself as having inherent worth... Excellent work, Jonny!

Subsequently, during the course of that day, I engaged in some administrative tasks, one of which involved reviewing my electronic correspondence. It was during this activity that I came across an e-mail addressed to me from a manager with whom I had professional interaction in the past. I accessed the inbox in order to review correspondence regarding tasks I had completed.

Jonathan, this required a significant amount of time to edit. "Please exercise greater attentiveness while perusing the text." A wave of distress abruptly overcame me.

You are performing subpar in your professional responsibilities, Jonny. You're useless. I was affirming to myself that I was unable to accomplish anything successfully.

The decisions and actions in my state were entirely influenced by the external sources from which I had obtained guidance. I had not employed personal agency and self-regulation in determining my self-perception. Undoubtedly, it is customary for individuals to experience fluctuations in their emotions, yet I consistently maintained such unwavering determination and concentration. I'm not alone.

Now, let us consider an illustration involving my acquaintance named Bill. Incidentally, I must clarify that I am not acquainted with an individual named Bill, and moreover, the narrative presented here has been creatively reconstructed. Bill was engaged in a romantic relationship with a young lady whom he held in high regard.

Upon receiving communication from her, he was filled with exhilaration and euphoria, experiencing a sense of unparalleled elation and joy.

However, in the absence of any communication from her, Bill consistently entertained pessimistic thoughts. He experienced a profound sense of inadequacy and despair, as he perceived a lack of affinity from those around him. He would never possess attractiveness among the female population.

Are you able to identify the issue presented by these individuals, one of whom happens to be myself? Their self-perceptions are heavily influenced by external factors. In the event of a favorable outcome, they experience a sense of self-assurance. If it fails to do so, then they are not capable. This situation is a perilous yet pervasive occurrence, I'm apprehensive to say.

Indeed, let us assign a designation to it, despite the likelihood that it has already been ascribed a name. How about: somethingelse-itis?

"You express great ingenuity, Jonny!" you exclaim. Awww, thanks.

In order to overcome a condition known as "somethingelse-itis," it is imperative that we enhance our self-esteem. By doing so, we can ensure that regardless of the circumstances we encounter, we consistently maintain a positive self-perception, even in situations that may be more challenging than others.

Let us cease the dissemination of narratives pertaining to:

I lack sufficient qualities to thrive independently without a romantic partner.

I do not deem myself satisfactory until I attain a certain count of followers.

I do not consider myself competent unless I attain the specified sum of money.

Such matters do not fall squarely within our purview. In light of our existing capabilities, what lies within the realm of our control? Our endeavors to pursue these objectives. Cultivate an affection for your work and behold the worth of your endeavors.

"This is within your sphere of influence." Learn to praise yourself. Similar to any other acquired ability, self-appreciation can be cultivated through learning.

Challenges and unfavorable results may present themselves as formidable obstacles. Therefore, please refrain from hastily concluding that any negative outcome equates to a mere acceptance of mediocrity after having given one's best effort.

You may still experience moments of disappointment; however, by cultivating a greater sense of self-appreciation and acknowledging your own efforts, the likelihood of encountering a decline in self-esteem is diminished.

Allow me to present a question for your consideration, which I myself have posed:

What would be the outcome if I were to depart and make an attempt, only to encounter further failure?

It is opportune to endeavor a fresh strategy. Seeking guidance from a mentor, coach, or knowledgeable individual can prove invaluable in this regard. Otherwise, there is a potential threat of succumbing to insanity due to the repetitiveness of our actions leading to unfruitful outcomes.

Action

Minimizing the extent of phone usage or social media engagement can contribute to the avoidance of seeking external validation. How can one derive self-satisfaction amidst the constant influx of external opinions regarding one's appearance, behavior, and so forth? I frequently receive advice on the proper methods of promoting my book, gaining access to numerous platforms, and effectively marketing my coaching enterprise.

I would advise against abruptly discontinuing your use, as this may lead to an increased inclination to check messages and engage with social media platforms for validation.

Alternatively, allocate specific periods during which you can abstain from using your cellular device and devote your attention to personal matters, as well as designate intervals for embarking on leisurely strolls.

A stroll unaccompanied by music, solely devoted to introspection and devoid of any electronic device, in an effort to fully immerse oneself in the immediate environment. It is truly advantageous for one's cognitive processes to have sufficient mental space. Even the inclusion of podcasts and music can disrupt this ambience and incite contemplation.

Techniques for cultivating presence:

● Mindfulness practice. There are many applications and methods that warrant consideration. I would suggest practicing nasal breathing for a duration of fifteen minutes.

● Setting aside brief moments throughout the day to engage in mindful observation of one's surroundings.

● Engaging in daily contemplative writing for a duration of ten minutes, reflecting on one's thoughts and emotions.

## Strategies For Overcoming Negative Thinking

In the end, should you find yourself entangled in such pessimistic rumination, there is a positive outcome awaiting you—a capacity to acquire the means to overcome it. There is no justification for you to remain trapped in those cycles of negative thinking. There is no rationale behind the compulsion for you to repeatedly confront those emotions; instead, you can acquire the ability to release them.

Overcoming pessimistic thoughts constitutes a pivotal aspect of this literary work. To cultivate a positive mindset, it is essential to acquire the skill of eliminating negative thoughts from your consciousness—a task that can prove quite challenging at times.

Nonetheless, accomplishing this task is attainable through a combination of expertise and a committed willingness to exert effort. This merely necessitates your embarkation on a journey of acquiring knowledge in order to ascertain your proficiency.

In this chapter, we will be discussing the fundamental principle of eliminating pessimistic thoughts. Once you acquire the ability to overcome them, rest assured that your future endeavors will yield significantly greater achievements. One can obtain the assurance that, in the end, they will triumph in their internal engagements, consequently enabling them to relinquish all of those negative emotions.

Over time, a buildup of negativity ensues within us, and it is only when we are capable of effectively discharging this negativity that we can truly commence our progress in life—a task that frequently proves to be challenging. Nevertheless, the procedure to accomplish this task is relatively straightforward. As you peruse this chapter, contemplate the manners in which you can initiate the adherence to these procedures for the purpose of eliminating pessimism from your existence as well. You are endeavoring to eliminate the unfavorable thoughts in order to create room in your life for the subsequent emergence of positive ones. It is of utmost importance, and if you are unable to accomplish it, you are likely to encounter difficulties. It is imperative that you ensure diligent effort in your work, and it is crucial that you adhere to these prescribed instructions.

After thoroughly reviewing the primary procedures for overcoming negativity, we shall now pause momentarily to contemplate the avenues through which you can initiate the pursuit of transformative actions in your life that will culminate in the desired outcomes. You will be presented with a selection of highly effective strategies to overcome negativity—and it is crucial to acknowledge that as you proceed further in the book, you will gain additional insights and knowledge. This book will provide you with the valuable opportunity to acquire knowledge and skills in cognitive restructuring, positivity, and a plethora of other areas.

Now, let's get started. Altering one's thought patterns need not be a daunting endeavor. Achieving this is attainable provided you demonstrate a willingness to allocate the necessary time and exert the requisite effort. You can do this. You will do this. Simply by possessing the desire and demonstrating diligent effort, you can achieve it. If you are able to fully commit yourself to cultivating these affirmative thoughts, you will discover that achieving a transformation of your mindset is far from insurmountable, contrary to your initial beliefs.

Recognize the Issue

First and foremost, it is imperative that you acknowledge the issue at hand. This holds true for virtually any matter requiring rectification; without acknowledging its presence, resolving it becomes impossible. Thus, by taking this crucial step, you will effectively eradicate it. It is imperative to ensure that, in the end, the manner in which one interacts with others is predominantly constructive. Having this objective inherently acknowledges that, at that particular juncture, there exists a need to mitigate any prevailing negativity in order to achieve success. You strive to ensure the attainment of the desired positivity and seek acknowledgment as a means to that end.

Desire to Alter" or "Wish to Amend

An additional condition for overcoming one's negativity is to possess a genuine intention to seek transformation initially. One must possess the desire to believe that one is capable of attaining a different state or altering one's approach to engaging with the world. This task is equally challenging as desiring change requires acknowledging the existence of a problem and its imperative to be rectified expeditiously. It is essential to possess the ability to devise an effective approach to harmonize with oneself and one's personal beliefs in order to effectively address the inner turmoil that arises from the realization that a significant portion of one's life and energy has been devoted to a pursuit one is now striving to overcome with utmost expediency and determination.

Accept Responsibility

The third phase in guaranteeing the attainment of the desired alteration is to ensure one is capable of assuming and embracing accountability. It is imperative that you take responsibility for your role in perpetuating the factors that hinder your progress. Once you are able to come to terms with and duly recognize the events that unfolded, as well as your own involvement in them, you can then commence the task of comprehending and assimilating the situation. You will have the capacity to enact meaningful transformations once you embrace both the authority and the accountability to initiate them. This may present challenges for certain individuals, but it is indeed possible to achieve.

# 10

## 5 Strategies for Developing a Formidable Level of Self-Assurance

Cultivating self-assurance is a continuous endeavor that demands unwavering resolve and vitality. Following are several guidelines to consider during the process of constructing your own:

Initial Step: Depart from the Familiar Territory

To cultivate unwavering confidence, it is imperative to exhibit a readiness to venture beyond the confines of your comfort zone in order to engage in extraordinary actions. You must awaken and cultivate the fervent desire within you to achieve greatness.

It is plausible that you possess an ingenious notion that could bring advantages to your organization, yet you are uncertain regarding the appropriate means to communicate this idea to your superior. It is possible that you harbor romantic feelings for someone that you have been hesitant to pursue.

The issue arising from failure to act upon these desires is the inherent risk of stagnation, resulting in an inability to progress. The undeniable reality is that by availing oneself of novel experiences, one is preventing fear from overshadowing their joy and fulfillment. You are merely reinforcing your penchant for staying within familiar confines. The cavity in which you have been occupying for an extended period of several decades.

Indeed, venturing into uncharted territory, with the inherent possibility of experiencing humiliation through unsuccessful attempts, can certainly evoke apprehension. However, upon further consideration, one may come to realize that it can be reduced to the acronym 'FEAR', which stands for False Evidence Appearing Real. What is the most dire outcome that could occur? Frequently, you tend to engage in excessive contemplation. Venturing beyond the confines of one's comfort zone can be undeniably intimidating, yet it remains imperative, should one seek to actualize their life's purpose and cultivate unwavering self-assurance. This could serve as an opportunity for you to demonstrate unequivocally your ability to accomplish any objective you sincerely commit yourself to.

In the final analysis, what is the utmost outcome that may transpire? One can collaborate with their supervisor and guide the organization towards achieving success, or alternatively, the supervisor may decline the suggestion. One could express interest in inviting the individual of interest on a date, and their response may yield either a positive or negative outcome. Additionally, this approach enables one to obtain a definitive answer in a time-efficient manner, avoiding excessive speculation. Regardless of the outcome, this scenario presents mutually beneficial circumstances.

The key to fostering unwavering self-assurance lies within oneself.

It is imperative to acknowledge that undertaking endeavors outside of one's comfort zone necessitates the establishment of incremental objectives, collectively contributing to achieving the overarching goal. Micro-objectives are simply indicative of diminutive fragments of the overarching objective at hand. When you systematically divide your larger objectives into manageable segments, their achievement becomes significantly more feasible, and you will derive considerable enjoyment throughout the process. Additionally, this will foster an increased sense of momentum, compelling you to persevere until you have successfully achieved your goal.

Therefore, it is inferred that you possess a business concept or plan that you desire to communicate to your superior but have yet to summon the bravery to do so. An alternative approach would be to divide your main objective into smaller objectives that ultimately yield comparable results. Begin by taking incremental measures, however minute they may be, in order to initiate progress. In lieu of embarking on a major undertaking and experiencing feelings of being overwhelmed, commencing with small steps will alleviate the pressure you may feel. By undertaking this approach, you facilitate a seamless comprehension and enable convenient subsequent actions.

So you harbor affection for that individual and lack the confidence to express your feelings. However, it is plausible that the individual in question is already in a committed relationship. Therefore, it is essential to initially build a rapport with them before delving into more profound matters. Prior to extending an invitation for a date, acquaint yourself with their character by initiating a brief conversation with the individual in question. Isn't that better? This does not appear to indicate any form of stalking on your part.

That being said, it is imperative to acknowledge that by establishing micro-goals, it enables one to venture beyond one's comfort zone. As you successfully accomplish your incremental objectives, you will come to the realization that each small triumph can contribute to the development of the self-assurance necessary to progress. Push yourself to engage in exceptional activities daily and observe how this enhances your self-assurance.

www.ingramcontent.com/pod-product-compliance
Lightning Source LLC
Chambersburg PA
CBHW052141110526
44591CB00012B/1810